Peter Rees

Why Do Swings Swing?

and other questions about forces

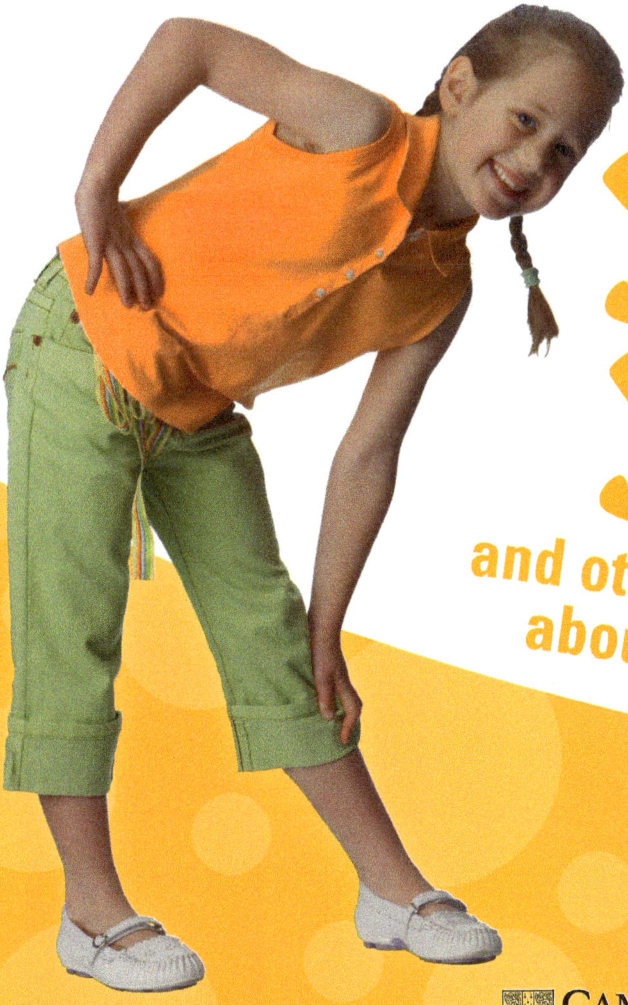

CAMBRIDGE
UNIVERSITY PRESS

Contents

Questions about movement 4

More questions about movement 6

It's a fact 8

Can you believe it? 10

Who found out? 12

It's quiz time! 14

Glossary 16

Questions about movement

Q: Why do swings swing?

A: Swings swing because a **force** moves them. A force is a push or a pull. When you push hard, the force is strong and the swing goes high.

Q: Why does my ball stop rolling?

A: Balls stop rolling because **friction** slows them down. Friction is when two things rub together, for example, a ball and the floor. A rough surface makes more friction than a smooth surface. That's why a ball rolls a longer distance on a wooden floor, and a shorter distance on a carpet.

Q: Why do swings stop swinging?

A: Swings stop swinging because friction between the air and a person slows the swing down. This is called **air resistance**. When you move your legs on the swing, you work against the friction and make the swing move. When you stop working against the friction, the swing stops swinging.

Cars have a special shape to reduce friction.

The ball rolls further on the wooden floor than on the carpeted floor because there is less friction.

More questions about movement

Q: What makes things change direction?

A: Things move in straight lines, unless a force makes them change direction. When you kick a football, the kick makes the ball change direction with a *pushing* force. When you pull the string on a balloon, the pull makes the balloon change direction with a *pulling* force.

Q: How do machines help us to move things?

A: Machines can turn weak forces into strong forces. There are many different kinds of machine. Simple machines can push, pull or lift. Hammers, ramps and wheels are simple machines.

Q: Why do things fall down?

A: Things fall down because of **gravity**. Gravity is the force that makes us stay on the ground. Gravity makes rain fall and rivers flow. With no gravity, everything would float away. When we jump up, we beat gravity, but only for a short time. What goes up must come down!

Lifting an aeroplane

An aeroplane stays in the air because of the wings. The wings bend the air. This gives the aeroplane **lift**. Lift is a force that pushes the aeroplane up.

It's a fact

> Wheels
Wheels are simple machines. They were invented about 5,500 years ago. Before then, people pulled heavy things on rollers.

> Cars
Simple machines can be attached to other machines to make new machines. A car is made of hundreds of simple machines working together.

> Levers
Levers are simple machines that lift. A seesaw is a lever. Your arms and legs are levers too!

> Wedges

Wedges are simple machines that split things or spread things apart. An axe is a wedge and so is a knife.

> Parachutes

Parachutes help people to land safely because the air pushes up against the parachute as the parachute falls, which slows it down. This is another example of air resistance.

> Earth's force

The Moon moves around the Earth at 1 kilometre per second. Earth's gravity stops the Moon from flying into space.

> Bicycle brakes

Bicycle brakes help you to stop safely because the lever makes the brake pads press the wheel. When the brake pad and the wheel rub against each other, they make friction, which slows down the wheel.

Can you believe it?

Energy for work

Energy is what something needs to make it move. Some machines get energy from petrol. Other machines get energy from batteries. We get energy from food. We store our energy as fat.

Building the pyramids

The Egyptians used simple machines to build the pyramids. They cut the stones with wedge-shaped tools. They used wooden rollers to pull the stones up huge ramps. Then levers lifted the stones into the right position.

Starting fires

Rub your hands together quickly. Do they feel warm? Friction between two objects makes heat. A long time ago people made fires by rubbing two sticks together. Today people use matches. The friction between the match and the matchbox makes fire.

Gravity versus magnets

Gravity is not a very strong force. Hold a magnet over some paperclips. What happens? The magnet pulls up the paperclips. The force of the small magnet is stronger than the gravity of the Earth.

The feather and the ball

Drop a feather and a ball at the same time. Which hits the ground first? The ball. Air resistance makes the feather move more slowly.

On the Moon, there is no friction because there is no air, so the feather and the ball would both hit the ground at the same time.

Forces website for kids:

http://www.kids-science-experiments.com/cat_gravity.html

Who Found out?

Levers: Archimedes

Archimedes (287–217 BCE) was a Greek scientist. He did not invent the lever, but he wrote about how it worked. In his book about levers he said, 'Give me a place to stand on and I will move the Earth.'

Gravity: Galileo Galilei

The Italian astronomer Galileo Galilei (1564–1642) was interested in many scientific things. It is said that he dropped two balls of different weights from the top of the Leaning Tower of Pisa to show that they would both drop at the same speed because the same force of gravity pulls them both.

Gravity: Isaac Newton

Isaac Newton (1642–1727) was a great British scientist. One day, he asked, 'What makes an apple fall from a tree?' He thought about this and found the answer: the force of gravity. This is the same force of gravity that holds the Moon in place and makes the planets **orbit** the Sun. He later used mathematics to work out the laws of gravity.

It's quiz time!

1   Match the things to the simple machines.

1. seesaw
2. knife
3. your arms

a) wedge
b) lever
c) lever

2   Match the words to the phrases to make sentences.

1. Parachutes
2. Brakes
3. Levers
4. Wedges
5. Rollers

a) are simple machines that lift.
b) help people to land safely.
c) were used to carry heavy things.
d) are machines that split things.
e) help you to stop safely.

3   Which is the odd one out? Why?

1. aeroplane, bird, car, bat _____
   _____

2. axe, knife, ball _____
   _____

3. push, bicycle, pull, gravity _____
   _____

4 Rearrange the words to make the sentences correct.

1. Balls stop friction because rolling slows them down.

   _____

   _____

2. A rough surface makes more surface than a smooth friction.

   _____

   _____

3. When you move your swing on a swing, you work against the friction and make the legs move.

   _____

   _____

4. When you kick a kick, the football makes the ball change direction with a pushing force.

   _____

   _____

5 Riddle. What is it?

We can beat it, but only for a short time. What goes up must come down.

_____

Glossary

air resistance: a force that slows down things as they move through air

energy: the power to act

force: a push or a pull that makes an object move, stop or change direction

friction: the rubbing of one object or surface against another

gravity: a force that pulls everything towards the ground

lever: simple machine shaped like a bar that moves up and down, used for lifting or pulling

lift: a lifting force that pushes an aeroplane up

orbit: to move around a planet or star

ramp: a sloping surface that goes from a high level to a lower level

wedge: simple machine with a sharp edge, used for splitting

wheel: round object used to make vehicles move